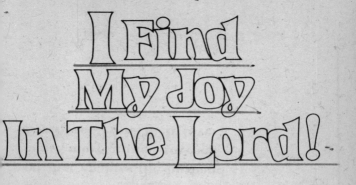

I Find My Joy In The Lord!

A TREASURY OF
FAVORITE BIBLICAL PRAYERS
FOR ALL THE SEASONS OF THE HEART

edited by
Roger J. Radley
from the Grail translation of the Psalms.

EMMAUS
BOOKS
PAULIST PRESS

For
my mother and father

©The Grail (England) 1963. Adapted from *The Psalms. A Singing Version* by Paulist Press by special arrangement with Wm. Collins Sons & Co. Ltd.

©1977 by
The Missionary Society
of St. Paul the Apostle
in the State of New York

Library of Congress
Catalog Card Number: 76-24446

ISBN: 0-8091-1990-0

Cover Design: Beehive Design Studio, Inc.

Photo Credit: Regina Siwek Shreter

Published by Paulist Press
Editorial Office: 1865 Broadway, N.Y., N.Y. 10023
Business Office: 545 Island Road, Ramsey, N.J. 07446

Printed and bound in the
United States of America

CONTENTS

Part I

When There Seems To Be No Hope
And I Need To Remember Your Past Blessings

Part II

When I Feel Alone and Need To See You

Part III

When I Feel Your Presence and Need To Thank You

Part IV

When I Am Weak and Need Your Strength

Part V

When I Recall Your Promises and Need To Live in Their Light

PART I

**When There Seems To Be No Hope
and I Need To Remember Your Past Blessings**

The Lord Said to Me:
"You Are My Son"

(Psalm 2)

1 Why this tumult among nations,
  among peoples this useless murmuring?
2 They arise, the kings of the earth,
  princes plot against the Lord and his Anointed.
3 'Come, let us break their fetters,
  come, let us cast off their yoke.'

4 He who sits in the heavens laughs;
  the Lord is laughing them to scorn.
5 Then he will speak in his anger,
  his rage will strike them with terror.
6 'It is I who have set up my king
  on Zion, my holy mountain.'

7 (I will announce the decree of the Lord:)

  The Lord said to me: 'You are my Son.
  It is I who have begotten you this day.
8 Ask and I shall bequeath you the nations,
  put the ends of the earth in your possession.
9 With a rod of iron you will break them,
  shatter them like a potter's jar.'

10 Now, O kings, understand,
  take warning, rulers of the earth;
11 serve the Lord with awe
  and trembling, pay him your homage
12 lest he be angry and you perish;
  for suddenly his anger will blaze.

  Blessed are they who put their trust in God.

His Justice Reaches Out
to Children's Children

(Psalm 102)

1 My soul, give thanks to the Lord,
   all my being, bless his holy name.
2 My soul, give thanks to the Lord
   and never forget all his blessings.

3 It is he who forgives all your guilt,
   who heals every one of your ills,
4 who redeems your life from the grave,
   who crowns you with love and compassion,
5 who fills your life with good things,
   renewing your youth like an eagle's.

6 The Lord does deeds of justice,
   gives judgment for all who are oppressed.
7 He made known his ways to Moses
   and his deeds to Israel's sons.

8 The Lord is compassion and love,
   slow to anger and rich in mercy.
9 His wrath will come to an end;
   he will not be angry for ever.
10 He does not treat us according to our sins
   nor repay us according to our faults.

11 For as the heavens are high above the earth
   so strong is his love for those who fear him.
12 As far as the east is from the west
   so far does he remove our sins.

13 As a father has compassion on his sons,
   the Lord has pity on those who fear him;

14 for he knows of what we are made,
   he remembers that we are dust.

15 As for man, his days are like grass;
   he flowers like the flower of the field;
16 the wind blows and he is gone
   and his place never sees him again.

17 But the love of the Lord is everlasting
   upon those who hold him in fear;
   his justice reaches out to children's children
18 when they keep his covenant in truth,
   when they keep his will in their mind.

19 The Lord has set his sway in heaven
   and his kingdom is ruling over all.
20 Give thanks to the Lord, all his angels,
   mighty in power, fulfilling his word,
   who heed the voice of his word.

21 Give thanks to the Lord, all his hosts,
   his servants who do his will.
22 Give thanks to the Lord, all his works,
   in every place where he rules.
   My soul, give thanks to the Lord!

He Calls Each One
by Its Name
(Psalm 146)

1 Alleluia!

Praise the Lord for he is good;
sing to our God for he is loving:
to him our praise is due.

2 The Lord builds up Jerusalem
and brings back Israel's exiles,
3 he heals the broken-hearted,
he binds up all their wounds.
4 He fixes the number of the stars;
he calls each one by its name.

5 Our Lord is great and almighty;
his wisdom can never be measured.
6 The Lord raises the lowly;
he humbles the wicked to the dust.
7 O sing to the Lord, giving thanks;
sing psalms to our God with the harp.

8 He covers the heavens with clouds;
he prepares the rain for the earth,
making mountains sprout with grass
and with plants to serve man's needs.
9 He provides the beasts with their food
and young ravens that call upon him.

10 His delight is not in horses
nor his pleasure in warriors' strength.
11 The Lord delights in those who revere him,
in those who wait for his love.

Your Hand Will Do All Things for Me

(Psalm 137)

1 I thank you, Lord, with all my heart,
  you have heard the words of my mouth.
  In the presence of the angels I will bless you.
2 I will adore before your holy temple.

  I thank you for your faithfulness and love
  which excel all we ever knew of you.
3 On the day I called, you answered;
  you increased the strength of my soul.

4 All earth's kings shall thank you
  when they hear the words of your mouth.
5 They shall sing of the Lord's ways:
  'How great is the glory of the Lord!'

6 The Lord is high yet he looks on the lowly
  and the haughty he knows from afar.
7 Though I walk in the midst of affliction
  you give me life and frustrate my foes.

  You stretch out your hand and save me,
  your hand 8 will do all things for me.
  Your love, O Lord, is eternal,
  discard not the work of your hands.

Standing Firm
For Ever and Ever

(Psalm 110)

1 Alleluia!

I will thank the Lord with all my heart
in the meeting of the just and their assembly.
2 Great are the works of the Lord;
to be pondered by all who love them.

3 Majestic and glorious his work,
his justice stands firm for ever.
4 He makes us remember his wonders.
The Lord is compassion and love.

5 He gives food to those who fear him;
keeps his covenant ever in mind.
6 He has shown his might to his people
by giving them the lands of the nations.

7 His works are justice and truth:
his precepts are all of them sure,
8 standing firm for ever and ever:
they are made in uprightness and truth.

9 He has sent deliverance to his people
and established his covenant for ever.
Holy his name, to be feared.

10 To fear the Lord is the first stage of wisdom;
all who do so prove themselves wise.
His praise shall last for ever!

With Justice
He Will Rule the World

(Psalm 95)

1 O sing a new song to the Lord,
  sing to the Lord, all the earth.
2 O sing to the Lord, bless his name.

  Proclaim his help day by day,
3 tell among the nations his glory
  and his wonders among all the peoples.

4 The Lord is great and worthy of praise,
  to be feared above all gods;
5 the gods of the heathens are naught.

  It was the Lord who made the heavens,
6 his are majesty and state and power
  and splendour in his holy place.

7 Give the Lord, you families of peoples,
  give the Lord glory and power,
8 give the Lord the glory of his name.

  Bring an offering and enter his courts,
9 worship the Lord in his temple.
  O earth, tremble before him.

10 Proclaim to the nations: 'God is king.'
  The world he made firm in its place;
  he will judge the peoples in fairness.

11 Let the heavens rejoice and earth be glad,
    let the sea and all within it thunder praise,
12 let the land and all it bears rejoice,
    all the trees of the wood shout for joy

13 at the presence of the Lord for he comes,
    he comes to rule the earth.
    With justice he will rule the world,
    he will judge the peoples with his truth.

For You Are Great and Do Marvellous Deeds

(Psalm 85)

1 Turn your ear, O Lord, and give answer
   for I am poor and needy.
2 Preserve my life, for I am faithful:
   save the servant who trusts in you.

3 You are my God, have mercy on me, Lord,
   for I cry to you all the day long.
4 Give joy to your servant, O Lord,
   for to you I lift up my soul.

5 O Lord, you are good and forgiving,
   full of love to all who call.
6 Give heed, O Lord, to my prayer
   and attend to the sound of my voice.

7 In the day of distress I will call
   and surely you will reply.
8 Among the gods there is none like you, O Lord;
   nor work to compare with yours.

9 All the nations shall come to adore you
   and glorify your name, O Lord:
10 for you are great and do marvellous deeds,
   you who alone are God.

11 Show me, Lord, your way
   so that I may walk in your truth.
   Guide my heart to fear your name.

12 I will praise you, Lord my God, with all my heart
    and glorify your name for ever;
13 for your love to me has been great:
    you have saved me from the depths of the grave.

14 The proud have risen against me;
    ruthless men seek my life:
    to you they pay no heed.

15 But you, God of mercy and compassion,
    slow to anger, O Lord,
    abounding in love and truth,
16 turn and take pity on me.

    O give your strength to your servant
    and save your handmaid's son.
17 Show me a sign of your favour
    that my foes may see to their shame
    that you console me and give me your help.

It Is You, O Lord, Who Will Take Us in Your Care

(Psalm 11)

2 Help, O Lord, for good men have vanished:
 truth has gone from the sons of men.
3 Falsehood they speak one to another,
 with lying lips, with a false heart.

4 May the Lord destroy all lying lips,
 the tongue that speaks high-sounding words,
5 those who say: 'Our tongue is our strength;
 our lips are our own, who is our master?'

6 'For the poor who are oppressed and the needy who
  groan
 I myself will arise,' says the Lord.
 'I will grant them the salvation for which they
  thirst.'

7 The words of the Lord are words without alloy,
 silver from the furnace, seven times refined.

8 It is you, O Lord, who will take us in your care
 and protect us for ever from this generation.
9 See how the wicked prowl on every side,
 while the worthless are prized highly by the sons of
  men.

Happy the Man
Who Trusts in You

(Psalm 83)

2 How lovely is your dwelling place,
   Lord, God of hosts.

3 My soul is longing and yearning,
   is yearning for the courts of the Lord.
   My heart and my soul ring out their joy
   to God, the living God.

4 The sparrow herself finds a home
   and the swallow a nest for her brood;
   she lays her young by your altars,
   Lord of hosts, my king and my God.

5 They are happy, who dwell in your house,
   for ever singing your praise.
6 They are happy, whose strength is in you,
   in whose hearts are the roads to Zion.

7 As they go through the Bitter Valley
   they make it a place of springs
   [the autumn rain covers it with blessings].
8 They walk with ever growing strength,
   they will see the God of gods in Zion.

9 O Lord God of hosts, hear my prayer,
   give ear, O God of Jacob.
10 Turn your eyes, O God, our shield,
   look on the face of your anointed.

11 One day within your courts
   is better than a thousand elsewhere.
   The threshold of the house of God
   I prefer to the dwellings of the wicked.

12 For the Lord God is a rampart, a shield;
   he will give us his favour and glory.
   The Lord will not refuse any good
   to those who walk without blame.

13 Lord, God of hosts,
   happy the man who trusts in you!

As for Me,
I Will Cry to God

(Psalm 54)

2 O God, listen to my prayer,
   do not hide from my pleading,
3 attend to me and reply;
   with my cares, I cannot rest.

   I tremble 4 at the shouts of the foe,
   at the cries of the wicked;
   for they bring down evil upon me.
   They assail me with fury.

5 My heart is stricken within me,
   death's terror is on me,
6 trembling and fear fall upon me
   and horror overwhelms me.

7 O that I had wings like a dove
   to fly away and be at rest.
8 So I would escape far away
   and take refuge in the desert.

9 I would hasten to find a shelter
   from the raging wind,
   from the destructive storm, O Lord,
10 and from their plotting tongues.

   For I can see nothing but violence
   and strife in the city.
11 Night and day they patrol
   high on the city walls.

It is full of wickedness and evil;
12 it is full of sin.
    Its streets are never free
    from tyranny and deceit.

13 If this had been done by an enemy
    I could bear his taunts.
    If a rival had risen against me,
    I could hide from him.

14 But it is you, my own companion,
    my intimate friend!
15 (How close was the friendship between us!)
    We walked together in harmony
    in the house of God.

16 May death fall suddenly upon them!
    Let them go to the grave:
    for wickedness dwells in their homes
    and deep in their hearts.

17 As for me, I will cry to God
    and the Lord will save me.
18 Evening, morning and at noon
    I will cry and lament.

19 He will deliver my soul in peace
    in the attack against me:
    for those who fight me are many,
18c but he hears my voice.

20 God will hear and will humble them,
    the eternal judge:
    for they will not amend their ways.
    They have no fear of God.

21 The traitor has turned against his friends;
   he has broken his word.
22 His speech is softer than butter,
   but war is in his heart.
   His words are smoother than oil,
   but they are naked swords.

23 Entrust your cares to the Lord
   and he will support you.
   He will never allow
   the just man to stumble.

24 But you, O God, will bring them down
   to the pit of death.
   Deceitful and bloodthirsty men
   shall not live half their days.

   O Lord, I will trust in you.

Wise Men and Fools Must Both Perish

(Psalm 48)

2 Hear this, all you peoples,
   give heed, all who dwell in the world,
3 men both low and high,
   rich and poor alike!

4 My lips will speak words of wisdom.
   My heart is full of insight.
5 I will turn my mind to a parable,
   with the harp I will solve my problem.

*   *   *

6 Why should I fear in evil days
   the malice of the foes who surround me,
7 men who trust in their wealth,
   and boast of the vastness of their riches?

8 For no man can buy his own ransom,
   or pay a price to God for his life.
9 The ransom of his soul is beyond him.
10 He cannot buy life without end,
   nor avoid coming to the grave.

11 He knows that wise men and fools must both perish
   and leave their wealth to others.
12 Their graves are their homes for ever,
   their dwelling place from age to age,
   though their names spread wide through the land.

13 In his riches, man lacks wisdom:
  he is like the beasts that are destroyed.

*   *   *

14 This is the lot of those who trust in themselves,
  who have others at their beck and call.
15 Like sheep they are driven to the grave,
  where death shall be their shepherd
  and the just shall become their rulers.

  With the morning their outward show vanishes
  and the grave becomes their home.
16 But God will ransom me from death
  and take my soul to himself.

17 Then do not fear when a man grows rich,
  when the glory of his house increases.
18 He takes nothing with him when he dies,
  his glory does not follow him below.

19 Though he flattered himself while he lived:
  'Men will praise me for all my success,'
20 yet he will go to join his fathers,
  who will never see the light any more.

21 In his riches, man lacks wisdom:
  he is like the beasts that are destroyed.

By This I Shall Know That You Are My Friend

(Psalm 40)

2 Happy the man who considers the poor and the
   weak.
  The Lord will save him in the day of evil,
3 will guard him, give him life, make him happy in the
   land
  and will not give him up to the will of his foes.
4 The Lord will help him on his bed of pain,
  he will bring him back from sickness to health.

5 As for me, I said: 'Lord, have mercy on me,
  heal my soul for I have sinned against you.'
6 My foes are speaking evil against me.
  'How long before he dies and his name be forgotten?'
7 They come to visit me and speak empty words,
  their hearts full of malice, they spread it abroad.

8 My enemies whisper together against me.
  They all weigh up the evil which is on me:
9 'Some deadly thing has fastened upon him,
  he will not rise again from where he lies.'
10 Thus even my friend, in whom I trusted,
  who ate my bread, has turned against me.

11 But you, O Lord, have mercy on me.
  Let me rise once more and I will repay them.
12 By this I shall know that you are my friend,
  if my foes do not shout in triumph over me.

13 If you uphold me I shall be unharmed
and set in your presence for evermore.

*   *   *

14 Blessed be the Lord, the God of Israel
from age to age. Amen. Amen.

The Lord Fills the Earth with His Love

(Psalm 32)

1 Ring out your joy to the Lord, O you just;
for praise is fitting for loyal hearts.

2 Give thanks to the Lord upon the harp,
with a ten-stringed lute sing him songs.
3 O sing him a song that is new,
play loudly, with all your skill.

4 For the word of the Lord is faithful
and all his works to be trusted.
5 The Lord loves justice and right
and fills the earth with his love.

6 By his word the heavens were made,
by the breath of his mouth all the stars.
7 He collects the waves of the ocean;
he stores up the depths of the sea.

8 Let all the earth fear the Lord,
all who live in the world revere him.
9 He spoke; and it came to be.
He commanded; it sprang into being.

10 He frustrates the designs of the nations,
he defeats the plans of the peoples.
11 His own designs shall stand for ever,
the plans of his heart from age to age.

12 They are happy, whose God is the Lord,
the people he has chosen as his own.
13 From the heavens the Lord looks forth,
he sees all the children of men.

14 From the place where he dwells he gazes
on all the dwellers on the earth,
15 he who shapes the hearts of them all
and considers all their deeds.

16 A king is not saved by his army,
nor a warrior preserved by his strength.
17 A vain hope for safety is the horse;
despite its power it cannot save.

18 The Lord looks on those who revere him,
on those who hope in his love,
19 to rescue their souls from death,
to keep them alive in famine.

20 Our soul is waiting for the Lord.
The Lord is our help and our shield.
21 In him do our hearts find joy.
We trust in his holy name.

22 May your love be upon us, O Lord,
as we place all our hope in you.

The Lord Is My Shepherd

(Psalm 23)

1 The Lord is my shepherd;
  there is nothing I shall want.
2 Fresh and green are the pastures where he gives me
    repose.
  Near restful waters he leads me,
3 to revive my drooping spirit.

  He guides me along the right path;
  he is true to his name.
4 If I should walk in the valley of darkness
  no evil would I fear.
  You are there with your crook and your staff;
  with these you give me comfort.

5 You have prepared a banquet for me
  in the sight of my foes.
  My head you have anointed with oil;
  my cup is overflowing.

6 Surely goodness and kindness shall follow me
  all the days of my life.
  In the Lord's own house shall I dwell
  for ever and ever.

My Life Is in Your Hands; Deliver Me

(Psalm 30)

2 In you, O Lord, I take refuge.
 Let me never be put to shame.
 In your justice, set me free,
3 hear me and speedily rescue me.

 Be a rock of refuge for me,
 a mighty stronghold to save me,
4 for you are my rock, my stronghold.
 For your name's sake, lead me and guide me.

5 Release me from the snares they have hidden
 for you are my refuge, Lord.
6 Into your hands I commend my spirit.
 It is you who will redeem me, Lord.

 O God of truth, 7 you detest
 those who worship false and empty gods.
8 As for me, I trust in the Lord:
 let me be glad and rejoice in your love.

 You who have seen my affliction
 and taken heed of my soul's distress,
9 have not handed me over to the enemy,
 but set my feet at large.

*   *   *

10 Have mercy on me, O Lord,
 for I am in distress.
 Tears have wasted my eyes,
 my throat and my heart.

11 For my life is spent with sorrow
   and my years with sighs.
   Affliction has broken down my strength
   and my bones waste away.

12 In the face of all my foes
   I am a reproach,
   an object of scorn to my neighbours
   and of fear to my friends.

   Those who see me in the street
   run far away from me.
13 I am like a dead man, forgotten,
   like a thing thrown away.

14 I have heard the slander of the crowd,
   fear is all around me,
   as they plot together against me,
   as they plan to take my life.

15 But as for me, I trust in you, Lord,
   I say: 'You are my God.
16 My life is in your hands, deliver me
   from the hands of those who hate me.

17 Let your face shine on your servant.
   Save me in your love.
18 Let me not be put to shame for I call you,
   let the wicked be shamed!

   Let them be silenced in the grave,
19 let lying lips be dumb,
   that speak haughtily against the just
   with pride and contempt.'

20 How great is the goodness, Lord,
    that you keep for those who fear you,
    that you show to those who trust you
    in the sight of men.

21 You hide them in the shelter of your presence
    from the plotting of men:
    you keep them safe within your tent
    from disputing tongues.

22 Blessed be the Lord who has shown me
    the wonders of his love
    in a fortified city.

23 'I am far removed from your sight'
    I said in my alarm.
    Yet you heard the voice of my plea
    when I cried for help.

24 Love the Lord, all you saints.
    He guards his faithful
    but the Lord will repay to the full
    those who act with pride.

25 Be strong, let your heart take courage,
    all who hope in the Lord.

PART II

When I Feel Alone and Need To See You

The Upright Shall See His Face

(Psalm 10)

1 In the Lord I have taken my refuge.
How can you say to my soul:
'Fly like a bird to its mountain.

2 See the wicked bracing their bow;
they are fixing their arrows on the string
to shoot upright men in the dark.
3 Foundations once destroyed, what can the just do?'

4 The Lord is in his holy temple,
the Lord, whose throne is in heaven.
His eyes look down on the world;
his gaze tests mortal men.

5 The Lord tests the just and the wicked:
the lover of violence he hates.
6 He sends fire and brimstone on the wicked;
he sends a scorching wind as their lot.

7 The Lord is just and loves justice:
the upright shall see his face.

I Cry Aloud to the Lord

(Psalm 3)

2 How many are my foes, O Lord!
. How many are rising up against me!
3 How many are saying about me:
'There is no help for him in God.'

4 But you, Lord, are a shield about me,
my glory, who lift up my head.
5 I cry aloud to the Lord.
He answers from his holy mountain.

6 I lie down to rest and I sleep.
I wake, for the Lord upholds me.
7 I will not fear even thousands of people
who are ranged on every side against me.

8 Arise, Lord; save me, my God,
you who strike all my foes on the mouth,
you who break the teeth of the wicked!
9 O Lord of salvation, bless your people!

He Is Our God

(Psalm 94)

1 Come, ring out our joy to the Lord;
  hail the rock who saves us.
2 Let us come before him, giving thanks,
  with songs let us hail the Lord.

3 A mighty God is the Lord,
  a great king above all gods.
4 In his hand are the depths of the earth;
  the heights of the mountains are his.
5 To him belongs the sea, for he made it
  and the dry land shaped by his hands.

6 Come in; let us bow and bend low;
  let us kneel before the God who made us
7 for he is our God and we
  the people who belong to his pasture,
  the flock that is led by his hand.

  O that to-day you would listen to his voice!
8 'Harden not your hearts as at Meribah,
  as on that day at Massah in the desert
9 when your fathers put me to the test;
  when they tried me, though they saw my work.

10 For forty years I was wearied of these people
  and I said: "Their hearts are astray,
  these people do not know my ways."
11 Then I took an oath in my anger:
  "Never shall they enter my rest." '

There Is No One
Who Takes My Part

(Psalm 141)

2 With all my voice I cry to the Lord,
  with all my voice I entreat the Lord.
3 I pour out my trouble before him;
  I tell him all my distress
4 while my spirit faints within me.
  But you, O Lord, know my path.

On the way where I shall walk
they have hidden a snare to entrap me.
5 Look on my right and see:
  there is no one who takes my part.
  I have no means of escape,
  not one who cares for my soul.

6 I cry to you, O Lord.
  I have said: 'You are my refuge,
  all I have in the land of the living.'
7 Listen, then, to my cry
  for I am in the depths of distress.

Rescue me from those who pursue me
for they are stronger than I.
8 Bring my soul out of this prison
  and then I shall praise your name.
  Around me the just will assemble
  because of your goodness to me.

Search Me, God, and Know My Heart

(Psalm 138)

1 O Lord, you search me and you know me,
2 you know my resting and my rising,
   you discern my purpose from afar.
3 You mark when I walk or lie down,
   all my ways lie open to you.

4 Before ever a word is on my tongue
   you know it, O Lord, through and through.
5 Behind and before you besiege me,
   your hand ever laid upon me.
6 Too wonderful for me, this knowledge,
   too high, beyond my reach.

7 O where can I go from your spirit,
   or where can I flee from your fáce?
8 If I climb the heavens, you are there.
   If I lie in the grave, you are there.

9 If I take the wings of the dawn
   and dwell at the sea's furthest end,
10 even there your hand would lead me,
   your right hand would hold me fast.

11 If I say: 'Let the darkness hide me
   and the light around me be night,'
12 even darkness is not dark for you
   and the night is as clear as the day.

13 For it was you who created my being,
   knit me together in my mother's womb.
14 I thank you for the wonder of my being,
   for the wonders of all your creation.

   Already you knew my soul,
15 my body held no secret from you
   when I was being fashioned in secret
   and moulded in the depths of the earth.

16 Your eyes saw all my actions,
   they were all of them written in your book;
   every one of my days was decreed
   before one of them came into being.

17 To me, how mysterious your thoughts,
   the sum of them not to be numbered!
18 If I count them, they are more than the sand;
   to finish, I must be eternal, like you.

19 O God, that you would slay the wicked!
   Men of blood, keep far away from me!
20 With deceit they rebel against you
   and set your designs at naught.

21 Do I not hate those who hate you,
   abhor those who rise against you?
22 I hate them with a perfect hate
   and they are foes to me.

23 O search me, God, and know my heart.
   O test me and know my thoughts.
24 See that I follow not the wrong path
   and lead me in the path of life eternal.

I Am Exhausted

(Psalm 6)

2 Lord, do not reprove me in your anger;
  punish me not, in your rage.
3 Have mercy on me, Lord, I have no strength;
  Lord, heal me, my body is racked;
4 my soul is racked with pain.

  But you, O Lord . . . how long?
5 Return, Lord, rescue my soul.
  Save me in your merciful love;
6 for in death no one remembers you;
  from the grave, who can give you praise?

7 I am exhausted with my groaning;
  every night I drench my pillow with tears;
  I bedew my bed with weeping.
8 My eye wastes away with grief;
  I have grown old surrounded by my foes.

9 Leave me, all you who do evil;
  for the Lord has heard my weeping.
10 The Lord has heard my plea;
  the Lord will accept my prayer.
11 All my foes will retire in confusion,
  foiled and suddenly confounded.

Can He Who Made the Ear Not Hear?

(Psalm 93)

1 O Lord, avenging God,
 avenging God, appear!
2 Judge of the earth, arise,
 give the proud what they deserve!

3 How long, O Lord, shall the wicked,
 how long shall the wicked triumph?
4 They bluster with arrogant speech;
 the evil-doers boast to each other.

5 They crush your people, Lord,
 they afflict the ones you have chosen.
6 They kill the widow and the stranger
 and murder the fatherless child.

7 And they say: 'The Lord does not see;
 the God of Jacob pays no heed.'
8 Mark this, most senseless of people;
 fools, when will you understand?

9 Can he who made the ear, not hear?
 Can he who formed the eye, not see?

10 Will he who trains nations, not punish?
 Will he who teaches men, not have knowledge?
11 (The Lord knows the thoughts of men.
 He knows they are no more than a breath.)

12 Happy the man whom you teach, O Lord,
   whom you train by means of your law:
13 to him you give peace in evil days
   while the pit is being dug for the wicked.

14 The Lord will not abandon his people
   nor forsake those who are his own:
15 for judgment shall again be just
   and all true hearts shall uphold it.

16 Who will stand up for me against the wicked?
   Who will defend me from those who do evil?
17 If the Lord were not to help me,
   I would soon go down into the silence.

18 When I think: 'I have lost my foothold',
   your mercy, Lord, holds me up.
19 When cares increase in my heart
   your consolation calms my soul.

20 Can judges who do evil be your friends?
   They do injustice under cover of law;
21 they attack the life of the just
   and condemn innocent blood.

22 As for me, the Lord will be a stronghold;
   my God will be the rock where I take refuge.
23 He will repay them for their wickedness,
   destroy them for their evil deeds.
   The Lord, our God, will destroy them.

God Was Their Rock

(Psalm 77)

1 Give heed, my people, to my teaching;
 turn your ear to the words of my mouth.
2 I will open my mouth in a parable
 and reveal hidden lessons of the past.

3 The things we have heard and understood,
 the things our fathers have told us
4 these we will not hide from their children
 but will tell them to the next generation:

the glories of the Lord and his might
 and the marvellous deeds he has done,
5 the witness he gave to Jacob,
 the law he established in Israel.

He gave a command to our fathers
 to make it known to their children
6 that the next generation might know it,
 the children yet to be born.

7 They too should arise and tell their sons
 that they too should set their hope in God
 and never forget God's deeds
 but keep every one of his commands:

8 so that they might not be like their fathers,
 a defiant and rebellious race,
 a race whose heart was fickle,
 whose spirit was unfaithful to God.

* * *

9 The sons of Ephraim, armed with the bow,
   turned back in the day of battle.
10 They failed to keep God's covenant
   and would not walk according to his law.

11 They forgot the things he had done,
   the marvellous deeds he had shown them.
12 He did wonders in the sight of their fathers,
   in Egypt, in the plains of Zoan.

13 He divided the sea and led them through
   and made the waters stand up like a wall.
14 By day he led them with a cloud:
   by night, with a light of fire.

15 He split the rocks in the desert.
   He gave them plentiful drink as from the deep.
16 He made streams flow out from the rock
   and made waters run down like rivers.

*   *   *

17 Yet still they sinned against him;
   they defied the Most High in the desert.
18 In their heart they put God to the test
   by demanding the food they craved.

19 They even spoke against God.
   They said: 'Is it possible for God
   to prepare a table in the desert?

20 It was he who struck the rock,
   water flowed and swept down in torrents.
   But can he also give us bread?
   Can he provide meat for his people?'

21 When he heard this the Lord was angry.
   A fire was kindled against Jacob,
   his anger rose against Israel
22 for having no faith in God;
   for refusing to trust in his help.

23 Yet he commanded the clouds above
   and opened the gates of heaven.
24 He rained down manna for their food,
   and gave them bread from heaven.

25 Mere men ate the bread of angels.
   He sent them abundance of food:
26 he made the east wind blow from heaven
   and roused the south wind by his might.

27 He rained food on them like dust,
   winged fowl like the sands of the sea.
28 He let it fall in the midst of their camp
   and all around their tents.

29 So they ate and had their fill;
   for he gave them all they craved.
30 But before they had sated their craving,
   while the food was still in their mouths,

31 God's anger rose against them.
   He slew the strongest among them,
   struck down the flower of Israel.

32 Despite this they went on sinning;
   they had no faith in his wonders:
33 so he ended their days like a breath
   and their years in sudden ruin.

34 When he slew them then they would seek him,
    return and seek him in earnest.
35 They would remember that God was their rock,
    God the Most High their redeemer.

36 But the words they spoke were mere flattery;
    they lied to him with their lips.
37 For their hearts were not truly with him;
    they were not faithful to his covenant.

38 Yet he who is full of compassion
    forgave their sin and spared them.
    So often he held back his anger
    when he might have stirred up his rage.

39 He remembered they were only men,
    a breath that passes never to return.

                    *   *   *

40 How often they defied him in the wilderness
    and caused him pain in the desert!

41 Yet again they put God to the test
    and grieved the Holy One of Israel.
42 They did not remember his deeds
    nor the day he saved them from the foe;

43 when he worked his miracles in Egypt,
    his wonders in the plains of Zoan:
44 when he turned their rivers into blood,
    made their streams impossible to drink.

45 He sent dog-flies against them to devour them
    and swarms of frogs to molest them.

46 he gave their crops to the grub,
   the fruit of their labour to the locust.

61 He gave his ark into captivity,
   his glorious ark into the hands of the foe.
62 He gave up his people to the sword,
   in his anger against his chosen ones.

63 So war devoured their young men,
   their maidens had no wedding songs;
64 their priests fell by the sword
   and their widows made no lament.

65 Then the Lord awoke as if from sleep,
   like a warrior overcome with wine.
66 He struck his foes from behind
   and put them to everlasting shame.

67 He rejected the tent of Joseph;
   he did not choose the tribe of Ephraim
68 but he chose the tribe of Judah,
   the hill of Zion which he loves.

69 He built his shrine like the heavens,
   or like the earth which he made firm for ever.
70 And he chose David his servant
   and took him away from the sheepfolds.

71 From the care of the ewes he called him
   to be shepherd of Jacob his people,
   of Israel his own possession.
72 He tended them with blameless heart,
   with discerning mind he led them.

Does God Forget His Mercy?

(Psalm 76)

2 I cry aloud to God,
   cry aloud to God that he may hear me.
3 In the day of my distress I sought the Lord.
   My hands were raised at night without ceasing;
   my soul refused to be consoled.
4 I remembered my God and I groaned.
   I pondered and my spirit fainted.

5 You withheld sleep from my eyes.
   I was troubled, I could not speak.
6 I thought of the days of long ago
   and remembered the years long past.
7 At night I mused within my heart.
   I pondered and my spirit questioned.

8 'Will the Lord reject us for ever?
   Will he show us his favour no more?
9 Has his love vanished for ever?
   Has his promise come to an end?
10 Does God forget his mercy
    or in anger withhold his compassion?'

11 I said: 'This is what causes my grief;
    that the way of the Most High has changed.'
12 I remember the deeds of the Lord,
    I remember your wonders of old,
13 I muse on all your works
    and ponder your mighty deeds.

14 Your ways, O God, are holy.

What god is great as our God?
15 You are the God who works wonders.
You showed your power among the peoples.
16 Your strong arm redeemed your people,
the sons of Jacob and Joseph.

17 The waters-saw you, O God,
the waters saw you and trembled;
the depths were moved with terror.
18 The clouds poured down rain,
the skies sent forth their voice;
your arrows flashed to and fro.

19 Your thunder rolled round the sky,
your flashes lighted up the world.
The earth was moved and trembled
20 when your way led through the sea,
your path through the mighty waters
and no one saw your footprints.

21 You guided your people like a flock
by the hand of Moses and Aaron.

Lord, Answer,
For Your Love Is Kind

(Psalm 68)

2 Save me, O God,
for the waters have risen to my neck.

3 I have sunk into the mud of the deep
and there is no foothold.
I have entered the waters of the deep
and the waves overwhelm me.

4 I am wearied with all my crying,
my throat is parched.
My eyes are wasted away
from looking for my God.

5 More numerous than the hairs on my head
are those who hate me without cause.
Those who attack me with lies
are too much for my strength.

How can I restore
what I have never stolen?
6 O God, you know my sinful folly;
my sins you can see.

7 Let those who hope in you not be put to shame
through me, Lord of hosts:
let not those who seek you be dismayed
through me, God of Israel.

8 It is for you that I suffer taunts,
   that shame covers my face,
9 that I have become a stranger to my brothers,
   an alien to my own mother's sons.
10 I burn with zeal for your house
   and taunts against you fall on me.

11 When I afflict my soul with fasting
   they make it a taunt against me.
12 When I put on sackcloth in mourning
   then they make me a byword,
13 the gossip of men at the gates,
   the subject of drunkards' songs.

14 This is my prayer to you,
   my prayer for your favour.
   In your great love, answer me, O God,
   with your help that never fails:
15 rescue me from sinking in the mud;
   save me from my foes.

   Save me from the waters of the deep
16 lest the waves overwhelm me.
   Do not let the deep engulf me
   nor death close its mouth on me.

17 Lord, answer, for your love is kind;
   in your compassion, turn towards me.
18 Do not hide your face from your servant;
   answer quickly for I am in distress.
19 Come close to my soul and redeem me;
   ransom me pressed by my foes.

20 You know how they taunt and deride me;
   my oppressors are all before you.

21 Taunts have broken my heart;
    I have reached the end of my strength.
    I looked in vain for compassion,
    for consolers; not one could I find.

22 For food they gave me poison;
    in my thirst they gave me vinegar to drink.
23 Let their table be a snare to them
    and their festive banquets a trap.
24 Let their eyes grow dim and blind;
    let their limbs tremble and shake.

25 Pour out your anger upon them,
    let the heat of your fury overtake them.
26 Let their camp be left desolate;
    let no one dwell in their tents:
27 for they persecute one whom you struck;
    they increase the pain of him you wounded.

28 Charge them with guilt upon guilt;
    let them never be found just in your sight.
29 Blot them out from the book of the living;
    do not enrol them among the just.
30 As for me in my poverty and pain
    let your help, O God, lift me up.

31 I will praise God's name with a song;
    I will glorify him with thanksgiving.
32 A gift pleasing God more than oxen,
    more than beasts prepared for sacrifice.

33 The poor when they see it will be glad
    and God-seeking hearts will revive;
34 for the Lord listens to the needy
    and does not spurn his servants in their chains.

35 Let the heavens and the earth give him praise,
   the sea and all its living creatures.

36 For God will bring help to Zion
   and rebuild the cities of Judah
   and men shall dwell there in possession.
37 The sons of his servants shall inherit it;
   those who love his name shall dwell there.

Many Are the Trials
of the Just Man

(Psalm 33)

2 I will bless the Lord at all times,
 his praise always on my lips;
3 in the Lord my soul shall make its boast.
 The humble shall hear and be glad.

4 Glorify the Lord with me,
 Together let us praise his name.
5 I sought the Lord and he answered me;
 from all my terrors he set me free.

6 Look towards him and be radiant;
 let your faces not be abashed.
7 This poor man called; the Lord heard him
 and rescued him from all his distress.

8 The angel of the Lord is encamped
 around those who revere him, to rescue them.
9 Taste and see that the Lord is good.
 He is happy who seeks refuge in him.

10 Revere the Lord, you his saints.
 They lack nothing, those who revere him.
11 Strong lions suffer want and go hungry
 but those who seek the Lord lack no blessing.

12 Come, children, and hear me
 that I may teach you the fear of the Lord.
13 Who is he who longs for life
 and many days, to enjoy his prosperity?

14 Then keep your tongue from evil
   and your lips from speaking deceit.
15 Turn aside from evil and do good;
   seek and strive after peace.

16 The Lord turns his face against the wicked
   to destroy their remembrance from the earth.
17 The Lord turns his eyes to the just
   and his ears to their appeal.

18 They call and the Lord hears
   and rescues them in all their distress.
19 The Lord is close to the broken-hearted;
   those whose spirit is crushed he will save.

20 Many are the trials of the just man
   but from them all the Lord will rescue him.
21 He will keep guard over all his bones,
   not one of his bones shall be broken.

22 Evil brings death to the wicked;
   those who hate the good are doomed.
23 The Lord ransoms the souls of his servants.
   Those who hide in him shall not be condemned.

PART III

**When I Feel Your Presence
and Need To Thank You**

You Have Put into My Heart
a Greater Joy

(Psalm 4)

2 When I call, answer me, O God of justice;
from anguish you released me, have mercy and hear
me!

3 O men, how long will your hearts be closed,
will you love what is futile and seek what is false?

4 It is the Lord who grants favours to those whom he
loves;
the Lord hears me whenever I call him.

5 Fear him; do not sin: ponder on your bed and be
still.
6 Make justice your sacrifice and trust in the Lord.

7 'What can bring us happiness?' many say.
Lift up the light of your face on us, O Lord.

8 You have put into my heart a greater joy
than they have from abundance of corn and new
wine.

9 I will lie down in peace and sleep comes at once
for you alone, Lord, make me dwell in safety.

Praise Him, Sun and Moon

(Psalm 148)

1 Alleluia!

Praise the Lord from the heavens,
praise him in the heights.
2 Praise him, all his angels,
praise him, all his host.

3 Praise him, sun and moon,
praise him, shining stars.
4 Praise him, highest heavens
and the waters above the heavens.

5 Let them praise the name of the Lord.
He commanded: they were made.
6 He fixed them for ever,
gave a law which shall not pass away.

7 Praise the Lord from the earth,
sea creatures and all oceans,
8 fire and hail, snow and mist,
stormy winds that obey his word;

9 all mountains and hills,
all fruit trees and cedars,
10 beasts, wild and tame,
reptiles and birds on the wing;

11 all earth's kings and peoples,
earth's princes and rulers;
12 young men and maidens,
old men together with children.

13 Let them praise the name of the Lord
   for he alone is exalted.
   The splendour of his name
   reaches beyond heaven and earth.

14 He exalts the strength of his people.
   He is the praise of all his saints,
   of the sons of Israel,
   of the people to whom he comes close.

   Alleluia!

His Love Endures For Ever

(Psalm 135)

1 Alleluia!
  O give thanks to the Lord for he is good,
  for his love endures for ever.
2 Give thanks to the God of gods,
  for his love endures for ever.
3 Give thanks to the Lord of lords,
  for his love endures for ever;

4 who alone has wrought marvellous works,
  for his love endures for ever;
5 whose wisdom it was made the skies,
  for his love endures for ever;
6 who fixed the earth firmly on the seas,
  for his love endures for ever.

7 It was he who made the great lights,
  for his love endures for ever,
8 the sun to rule in the day,
  for his love endures for ever,
9 the moon and stars in the night,
  for his love endures for ever.

10 The first-born of the Egyptians he smote,
  for his love endures for ever.
11 He brought Israel out from their midst,
  for his love endures for ever;
12 arm outstretched, with power in his hand,
  for his love endures for ever.

13 He divided the Red Sea in two,

for his love endures for ever;

14 he made Israel pass through the midst,
for his love endures for ever;

15 he flung Pharaoh and his force in the sea,
for his love endures for ever.

16 Through the desert his people he led,
for his love endures for ever.

17 Nations in their greatness he struck,
for his love endures for ever.

18 Kings in their splendour he slew,
for his love endures for ever.

19 Sihon, king of the Amorites,
for his love endures for ever;

20 and Og, the king of Bashan,
for his love endures for ever.

21 He let Israel inherit their land,
for his love endures for ever.

22 On his servant their land he bestowed,
for his love endures for ever.

23 He remembered us in our distress,
for his love endures for ever.

24 And he snatched us away from our foes,
for his love endures for ever.

25 He gives food to all living things,
for his love endures for ever.

26 To the God of heaven give thanks,
for his love endures for ever.

Bless the Lord Through the Night

(Psalm 133)

1 O come, bless the Lord,
   all you who serve the Lord,
   who stand in the house of the Lord,
   in the courts of the house of our God.

2 Lift up your hands to the holy place
   and bless the Lord through the night.

3 May the Lord bless you from Zion,
   he who made both heaven and earth.

Let Us Go to the Place of His Dwelling

(Psalm 131)

1 O Lord, remember David
  and all the many hardships he endured,
2 the oath he swore to the Lord,
  his vow to the Strong One of Jacob.

3 'I will not enter the house where I live
  nor go to the bed where I rest.
4 I will give no sleep to my eyes,
  to my eyelids I will give no slumber
5 till I find a place for the Lord,
  a dwelling for the Strong One of Jacob.'

6 At Ephrata we heard of the ark;
  we found it in the plains of Yearim.
7 'Let us go to the place of his dwelling;
  let us go to kneel at his footstool.'

8 Go up, Lord, to the place of your rest,
  you and the ark of your strength.
9 Your priests shall be clothed with holiness:
  your faithful shall ring out their joy.
10 For the sake of David your servant
  do not reject your anointed.

11 The Lord swore an oath to David;
  he will not go back on his word:
  'A son, the fruit of your body,
  will I set upon your throne.

12 If they keep my covenant in truth
   and my laws that I have taught them,
   their sons also shall rule
   on your throne from age to age.'

13 For the Lord has chosen Zion;
   he has desired it for his dwelling:
14 'This is my resting-place for ever,
   here have I chosen to live.

15 I will greatly bless her produce,
   I will fill her poor with bread.
16 I will clothe her priests with salvation
   and her faithful shall ring out their joy.

17 There David's stock will flower:
   I will prepare a lamp for my anointed.
18 I will cover his enemies with shame
   but on him my crown shall shine.'

I Will Sing to the Lord
All My Life

(Psalm 103)

1 Bless the Lord, my soul!
  Lord God, how great you are,
  clothed in majesty and glory,
2 wrapped in light as in a robe!

*   *   *

You stretch out the heavens like a tent.
3 Above the rains you build your dwelling.
  You make the clouds your chariot,
  you walk on the wings of the wind,
4 you make the winds your messengers
  and flashing fire your servants.

5 You founded the earth on its base,
  to stand firm from age to age.
6 You wrapped it with the ocean like a cloak:
  the waters stood higher than the mountains.

7 At your threat they took to flight;
  at the voice of your thunder they fled.
8 They rose over the mountains and flowed down
  to the place which you had appointed.
9 You set limits they might not pass
  lest they return to cover the earth.

10 You make springs gush forth in the valleys:
   they flow in between the hills.

11 They give drink to all the beasts of the field;
   the wild-asses quench their thirst.
12 On their banks dwell the birds of heaven;
   from the branches they sing their song.

13 From your dwelling you water the hills;
   earth drinks its fill of your gift.
14 You make the grass grow for the cattle
   and the plants to serve man's needs,

   that he may bring forth bread from the earth
15 and wine to cheer man's heart;
   oil, to make his face shine
   and bread to strengthen man's heart.

16 The trees of the Lord drink their fill,
   the cedars he planted on Lebanon;
17 there the birds build their nests:
   on the tree-top the stork has her home.
18 The goats find a home on the mountains
   and rabbits hide in the rocks.

19 You made the moon to mark the months;
   the sun knows the time for its setting.
20 When you spread the darkness it is night
   and all the beasts of the forest creep forth.
21 The young lions roar for their prey
   and ask their food from God.

22 At the rising of the sun they steal away
   and go to rest in their dens.
23 Man goes forth to his work,
   to labour till evening falls.

24 How many are your works, O Lord!

In wisdom you have made them all.
The earth is full of your riches.

25 There is the sea, vast and wide,
with its moving swarms past counting,
living things great and small.
26 The ships are moving there
and the monsters you made to play with.

27 All of these look to you
to give them their food in due season.
28 You give it, they gather it up:
you open your hand, they have their fill.

29 You hide your face, they are dismayed;
you take back your spirit, they die,
returning to the dust from which they came.
30 You send forth your spirit, they are created;
and you renew the face of the earth.

31 May the glory of the Lord last for ever!
May the Lord rejoice in his works!
32 He looks on the earth and it trembles;
the mountains send forth smoke at his touch.

33 I will sing to the Lord all my life,
make music to my God while I live.
34 May my thoughts be pleasing to him.
I find my joy in the Lord.
35 Let sinners vanish from the earth
and the wicked exist no more.

Bless the Lord, my soul.

Cry Out with Joy
to the Lord

(Psalm 99)

1 Cry out with joy to the Lord, all the earth.
2 Serve the Lord with gladness.
  Come before him, singing for joy.

3 Know that he, the Lord, is God.
  He made us, we belong to him,
  we are his people, the sheep of his flock.

4 Go within his gates, giving thanks.
  Enter his courts with songs of praise.
  Give thanks to him and bless his name.

5 Indeed, how good is the Lord,
  eternal his merciful love.
  He is faithful from age to age.

The Lord Holds a Cup
in His Hand

(Psalm 74)

2 We give thanks to you, O God,
   we give thanks and call upon your name.
   We recount your wonderful deeds.

*　　*　　*

3 'When I reach the appointed time,
   then I will judge with justice.
4 Though the earth and all who dwell in it may rock,
   it is I who uphold its pillars.

5 To the boastful I say: "Do not boast,"
   to the wicked: "Do not flaunt your strength,
6 do not flaunt your strength on high.
   Do not speak with insolent pride."'

7 For neither from the east nor from the west,
   nor from desert or mountains comes judgment,
8 but God himself is the judge.
   One he humbles, another he exalts.

9 The Lord holds a cup in his hand,
   full of wine, foaming and spiced.
   He pours it; they drink it to the dregs:
   all the wicked on the earth must drain it.

10 As for me, I will rejoice for ever
   and sing psalms to Jacob's God.
11 He shall break the power of the wicked,
   while the strength of the just shall be exalted.

Let All the Peoples Praise You

(Psalm 66)

2 O God, be gracious and bless us
   and let your face shed its light upon us.
3 So will your ways be known upon earth
   and all nations learn your saving help.

4 Let the peoples praise you, O God;
   let all the peoples praise you.

5 Let the nations be glad and exult
   for you rule the world with justice.
   With fairness you rule the peoples,
   you guide the nations on earth.

6 Let the peoples praise you, O God;
   let all the peoples praise you.

7 The earth has yielded its fruit
   for God, our God, has blessed us.
8 May God still give us his blessing
   till the ends of the earth revere him.

Let the peoples praise you, O God;
let all the peoples praise you.

I Was Helped,
My Heart Rejoices

(Psalm 27)

1 To you, O Lord, I call,
  my rock, hear me.
  If you do not heed I shall become
  like those in the grave.

2 Hear the voice of my pleading
  as I call for help,
  as I lift up my hands in prayer
  to your holy place.

3 Do not drag me away with the wicked,
  with the evil-doers,
  who speak words of peace to their neighbours
  but with evil in their hearts.

4 Repay them as their actions deserve
  and the malice of their deeds.
  Repay them for the work of their hands;
  give them their deserts.
5 For they ignore the deeds of the Lord
  and the work of his hands.
  (May he ruin them and never rebuild them.)

6 Blessed be the Lord for he has heard
  my cry, my appeal.
7 The Lord is my strength and my shield;
  in him my heart trusts.
  I was helped, my heart rejoices
  and I praise him with my song.

8 The Lord is the strength of his people,
  a fortress where his anointed find help.
9 Save your people; bless Israel your heritage.
  Be their shepherd and carry them for ever.

These Things the Lord Has Done

(Psalm 21)

2 My God, my God, why have you forsaken me?
   You are far from my plea and the cry of my distress.
3 O my God, I call by day and you give no reply;
   I call by night and I find no peace.

4 Yet you, O God, are holy,
   enthroned on the praises of Israel.
5 In you our fathers put their trust;
   they trusted and you set them free.
6 When they cried to you, they escaped.
   In you they trusted and never in vain.

7 But I am a worm and no man,
   the butt of men, laughing-stock of the people.
8 All who see me deride me.
   They curl their lips, they toss their heads.
9 'He trusted in the Lord, let him save him;
   let him release him if this is his friend.'

10 Yes, it was you who took me from the womb,
   entrusted me to my mother's breast.
11 To you I was committed from my birth,
   from my mother's womb you have been my God.
12 Do not leave me alone in my distress;
   come close, there is none else to help.

13 Many bulls have surrounded me,
   fierce bulls of Bashan close me in.
14 Against me they open wide their jaws,
   like lions, rending and roaring.

15 Like water I am poured out,
    disjointed are all my bones.
    My heart has become like wax,
    it is melted within my breast.

16 Parched as burnt clay is my throat,
    my tongue cleaves to my jaws.

17 Many dogs have surrounded me,
    a band of the wicked beset me.
    They tear holes in my hands and my feet
16c and lay me in the dust of death.

18 I can count every one of my bones.
    These people stare at me and gloat;
19 they divide my clothing among them.
    They cast lots for my robe.

20 O Lord, do not leave me alone,
    my strength, make haste to help me!
21 Rescue my soul from the sword,
    my life from the grip of these dogs.
22 Save my life from the jaws of these lions,
    my poor soul from the horns of these oxen.

23 I will tell of your name to my brethren
    and praise you where they are assembled.
24 'You who fear the Lord give him praise;
    all sons of Jacob, give him glory.
    Revere him, Israel's sons.

25 For he has never despised
    nor scorned the poverty of the poor.
    From him he has not hidden his face,
    but he heard the poor man when he cried.'

26 You are my praise in the great assembly.
My vows I will pay before those who fear him.
27 The poor shall eat and shall have their fill.
They shall praise the Lord, those who seek him.
May their hearts live for ever and ever!

28 All the earth shall remember and return to the Lord,
all families of the nations worship before him
29 for the kingdom is the Lord's; he is ruler of the nations.
30 They shall worship him, all the mighty of the earth;
before him shall bow all who go down to the dust.

And my soul shall live for him, 31 my children serve him.
They shall tell of the Lord to generations yet to come,
32 declare his faithfulness to peoples yet unborn:
'These things the Lord has done.'

My Heart Rejoices,
My Soul Is Glad

(Psalm 15)

1 Preserve me, God, I take refuge in you.
2 I say to the Lord: 'You are my God.
My happiness lies in you alone.'

3 He has put into my heart a marvellous love
for the faithful ones who dwell in his land.
4 Those who choose other gods increase their sorrows.
Never will I offer their offerings of blood.
Never will I take their name upon my lips.

5 O Lord, it is you who are my portion and cup;
it is you yourself who are my prize.
6 The lot marked out for me is my delight:
welcome indeed the heritage that falls to me!

7 I will bless the Lord who gives me counsel,
who even at night directs my heart.
8 I keep the Lord ever in my sight:
since he is at my right hand, I shall stand firm.

9 And so my heart rejoices, my soul is glad;
even my body shall rest in safety.
10 For you will not leave my soul among the dead,
nor let your beloved know decay.

11 You will show me the path of life,
the fullness of joy in your presence,
at your right hand happiness for ever.

Sing a New Song to the Lord

(Psalm 97)

1 Sing a new song to the Lord
  for he has worked wonders.
  His right hand and his holy arm
  have brought salvation.

2 The Lord has made known his salvation;
  has shown his justice to the nations.
3 He has remembered his truth and love
  for the house of Israel.

  All the ends of the earth have seen
  the salvation of our God.
4 Shout to the Lord, all the earth,
  ring out your joy.

5 Sing psalms to the Lord with the harp
  with the sound of music.
6 With trumpets and the sound of the horn
  acclaim the King, the Lord.

*   *   *

7 Let the sea and all within it, thunder;
  the world, and all its peoples.
8 Let the rivers clap their hands
  and the hills ring out their joy

9 at the presence of the Lord: for he comes,
  he comes to rule the earth.
  He will rule the world with justice
  and the peoples with fairness.

PART IV

**When I Am Weak
and Need Your Strength**

Lead Me, Lord, in Your Justice

(Psalm 5)

2 To my words give ear, O Lord,
   give heed to my groaning.
3 Attend to the sound of my cries,
   my King and my God.

It is you whom I invoke, 4 O Lord.
In the morning you hear me;
in the morning I offer you my prayer,
watching and waiting.

5 You are no God who loves evil;
   no sinner is your guest.
6 The boastful shall not stand their ground
   before your face.

7 You hate all who do evil:
   you destroy all who lie.
   The deceitful and bloodthirsty man
   the Lord detests.

8 But I through the greatness of your love
   have access to your house.
   I bow down before your holy temple,
   filled with awe.

9 Lead me, Lord, in your justice,
   because of those who lie in wait;
   make clear your way before me.

10 No truth can be found in their mouths,
    their heart is all mischief,
    their throat a wide-open grave,
    all honey their speech.

11 Declare them guilty, O God.
    Let them fail in their designs.
    Drive them out for their many offences;
    for they have defied you.

12 All those you protect shall be glad
    and ring out their joy.
    You shelter them; in you they rejoice,
    those who love your name.

13 It is you who bless the just man, Lord:
    you surround him with favour as with a shield.

A Humbled, Contrite Heart
You Will Not Spurn

(Psalm 50)

3 Have mercy on me, God, in your kindness.
  In your compassion blot out my offence.
4 O wash me more and more from my guilt
  and cleanse me from my sin.

5 My offences truly I know them;
  my sin is always before me.
6 Against you, you alone, have I sinned;
  what is evil in your sight I have done.

That you may be justified when you give sentence
  and be without reproach when you judge
7 O see, in guilt I was born,
  a sinner was I conceived.

8 Indeed you love truth in the heart;
  then in the secret of my heart teach me wisdom.
9 O purify me, then I shall be clean;
  O wash me, I shall be whiter than snow.

10 Make me hear rejoicing and gladness,
  that the bones you have crushed may thrill.
11 From my sins turn away your face
  and blot out all my guilt.

12 A pure heart create for me, O God,
  put a steadfast spirit within me.
13 Do not cast me away from your presence,
  nor deprive me of your holy spirit.

14 Give me again the joy of your help;
   with a spirit of fervour sustain me,
15 that I may teach transgressors your ways
   and sinners may return to you.

16 O rescue me, God, my helper,
   and my tongue shall ring out your goodness.
17 O Lord, open my lips
   and my mouth shall declare your praise.

18 For in sacrifice you take no delight,
   burnt offering from me you would refuse,
19 my sacrifice, a contrite spirit.,
   A humbled, contrite heart you will not spurn.

20 In your goodness, show favour to Zion:
   rebuild the walls of Jerusalem.
21 Then you will be pleased with lawful sacrifice,
   (burnt offerings wholly consumed),
   then you will be offered young bulls on your altar.

Bring Us Together
From Among the Nations

(Psalm 105)

1 Alleluia!

O give thanks to the Lord for he is good;
for his love endures for ever
2 Who can tell the Lord's mighty deeds?
Who can recount all his praise?

3 They are happy who do what is right,
who at all times do what is just.
4 O Lord, remember me
out of the love you have for your people.

Come to me, Lord, with your help
5 that I may see the joy of your chosen ones
and may rejoice in the gladness of your nation
and share the glory of your people.

6 Our sin is the sin of our fathers;
we have done wrong, our deeds have been evil.
7 Our fathers when they were in Egypt
paid no heed to your wonderful deeds.

They forgot the greatness of your love;
at the Red Sea defied the Most High.
8 Yet he saved them for the sake of his name,
in order to make known his power.

9 He threatened the Red Sea; it dried up
and he led them through the deep as through the
desert.

10 He saved them from the hand of the foe;
   he saved them from the grip of the enemy.

11 The waters covered their oppressors;
   not one of them was left alive.
12 Then they believed in his words:
   then they sang his praises.

13 But they soon forgot his deeds
   and would not wait upon his will.
14 They yielded to their cravings in the desert
   and put God to the test in the wilderness.

15 He granted them the favour they asked
   and sent disease among them.
16 Then they rebelled, envious of Moses
   and of Aaron, who was holy to the Lord.

17 The earth opened and swallowed up Dathan
   and buried the clan of Abiram.
18 Fire blazed up against their clan
   and flames devoured the rebels.

19 They fashioned a calf at Horeb
   and worshipped an image of metal,
20 exchanging the God who was their glory
   for the image of a bull that eats grass.

21 They forgot the God who was their saviour,
   who had done such great things in Egypt,
22 such portents in the land of Ham,
   such marvels at the Red Sea.

23 For this he said he would destroy them,
   but Moses, the man he had chosen,

stood in the breach before him,
to turn back his anger from destruction.

24 Then they scorned the land of promise:
they had no faith in his word.
25 They complained inside their tents
and would not listen to the voice of the Lord.

26 So he raised his hand to swear an oath
that he would lay them low in the desert;
27 would scatter their sons among the nations
and disperse them throughout the lands.

28 They bowed before the Baal of Peor;
ate offerings made to lifeless gods.
29 They roused him to anger with their deeds
and a plague broke out among them.

30 Then Phinehas stood up and intervened.
Thus the plague was ended
31 and this was counted in his favour
from age to age for ever.

32 They provoked him at the waters of Meribah.
Through their fault it went ill with Moses;
33 for they made his heart grow bitter
and he uttered words that were rash.

34 They failed to destroy the peoples
as the Lord had given command,
35 but instead they mingled with the nations
and learned to act as they did.

36 They worshipped the idols of the nations
and these became a snare to entrap them.
37 They even offered their own sons
and their daughters in sacrifice to demons.

38 They shed the blood of the innocent,
   the blood of their sons and daughters
   whom they offered to the idols of Canaan.
   The land was polluted with blood.

39 So they defiled themselves by their deeds
   and broke their marriage bond with the Lord
40 till his anger blazed against his people:
   he was filled with horror at his chosen ones.

41 So he gave them into the hand of the nations
   and their foes became their rulers.
42 Their enemies became their oppressors;
   they were subdued beneath their hand.

43 Time after time he rescued them,
   but in their malice they dared to defy him
   and sank low through their guilt.
44 In spite of this he paid heed to their distress,
   so often as he heard their cry.

45 For their sake he remembered his covenant.
   In the greatness of his love he relented
46 and he let them be treated with mercy
   by all who held them captive.

47 O Lord, our God, save us!
   Bring us together from among the nations
   that we may thank your holy name
   and make it our glory to praise you.

*   *   *

48 Blessed be the Lord, God of Israel,
   for ever, from age to age.
   Let all the people cry out:
   'Amen! Amen! Alleluia!'

Such a Man Will Stand Firm For Ever

(Psalm 14)

1 Lord, who shall be admitted to your tent
  and dwell on your holy mountain?

2 He who walks without fault;
  he who acts with justice
  and speaks the truth from his heart;
3 he who does not slander with his tongue;

  he who does no wrong to his brother,
  who casts no slur on his neighbour,
4 who holds the godless in disdain,
  but honours those who fear the Lord;

  he who keeps his pledge, come what may;
5 who takes no interest on a loan
  and accepts no bribes against the innocent.
  Such a man will stand firm for ever.

They Did His Will;
They Kept the Law

(Psalm 98)

1 The Lord is king; the peoples tremble.
  He is throned on the cherubim; the earth quakes.
2 The Lord is great in Zion.

  He is supreme over all the peoples.
3 Let them praise his name, so terrible and great.
  he is holy, *4* full of power.

  You are a king who loves what is right;
  you have established equity, justice and right;
  you have established them in Jacob.

5 Exalt the Lord our God;
  bow down before Zion, his footstool.
  He the Lord is holy.

6 Among his priests were Aaron and Moses,
  among those who invoked his name was Samuel.
  They invoked the Lord and he answered.

7 To them he spoke in the pillar of cloud.
  They did his will; they kept the law,
  which he, the Lord, had given.

8 O Lord our God, you answered them.
  For them you were a God who forgives;
  yet you punished all their offences.

9 Exalt the Lord our God;
  bow down before his holy mountain
  for the Lord our God is holy.

In Silence and Peace

(Psalm 130)

1 O Lord, my heart is not proud
nor haughty my eyes.
I have not gone after things too great
nor marvels beyond me.

2 Truly I have set my soul
in silence and peace.
A weaned child on its mother's breast,
even so is my soul.

3 O Israel, hope in the Lord
both now and for ever.

I Put My Trust in You

(Psalm 142)

1 Lord, listen to my prayer:
turn your ear to my appeal.
You are faithful, you are just; give answer.
2 Do not call your servant to judgment
for no one is just in your sight.

3 The enemy pursues my soul;
he has crushed my life to the ground;
he has made me dwell in darkness
like the dead, long forgotten.
4 Therefore my spirit fails;
my heart is numb within me.

5 I remember the days that are past:
I ponder all your works.
I muse on what your hand has wrought
6 and to you I stretch out my hands.
Like a parched land my soul thirsts for you.

7 Lord, make haste and answer;
for my spirit fails within me.
Do not hide your face
lest I become like those in the grave.

8 In the morning let me know your love
for I put my trust in you.
Make me know the way I should walk:
to you I lift up my soul.

9 Rescue me, Lord, from my enemies;
   I have fled to you for refuge.
10 Teach me to do your will
   for you, O Lord, are my God.
   Let your good spirit guide me
   in ways that are level and smooth.

11 For your name's sake, Lord, save my life;
   in your justice save my soul from distress.
12 In your love make an end of my foes;
   destroy all those who oppress me
   for I am your servant, O Lord.

Light Shines Forth
for the Just

(Psalm 96)

1 The Lord is king, let earth rejoice,
   let all the coastlands be glad.
2 Cloud and darkness are his raiment;
   his throne, justice and right.

3 A fire prepares his path;
   it burns up his foes on every side.
4 His lightnings light up the world,
   the earth trembles at the sight.

5 The mountains melt like wax
   before the Lord of all the earth.
6 The skies proclaim his justice;
   all peoples see his glory.

7 Let those who serve idols be ashamed,
   those who boast of their worthless gods.
   All you spirits, worship him.

8 Zion hears and is glad;
   the people of Judah rejoice
   because of your judgments, O Lord.

9 For you indeed are the Lord
   most high above all the earth,
   exalted far above all spirits.

10 The Lord loves those who hate evil:
   he guards the souls of his saints;
   he sets them free from the wicked.

11 Light shines forth for the just
   and joy for the upright of heart.
12 Rejoice, you just, in the Lord;
   give glory to his holy name.

The Foolish Man Cannot Know This

(Psalm 91)

2 It is good to give thanks to the Lord,
  to make music to your name, O Most High,
3 to proclaim your love in the morning
  and your truth in the watches of the night,
4 on the ten-stringed lyre and the lute,
  with the murmuring sound of the harps.

5 Your deeds, O Lord, have made me glad;
  for the work of your hands I shout with joy.
6 O Lord, how great are your works!
  How deep are your designs!
7 The foolish man cannot know this
  and the fool cannot understand.

8 Though the wicked spring up like grass
  and all who do evil thrive:
  they are doomed to be eternally destroyed.
9 But you, Lord, are eternally on high.
10 See how your enemies perish;
  all doers of evil are scattered.

11 To me you give the wild-ox's strength;
  you anoint me with the purest oil.
12 My eyes looked in triumph on my foes;
  my ears heard gladly of their fall.
13 The just will flourish like the palm-tree
  and grow like a Lebanon cedar.

14 Planted in the house of the Lord
   they will flourish in the courts of our God,
15 still bearing fruit when they are old,
   still full of sap, still green,
16 to proclaim that the Lord is just.
   In him, my rock, there is no wrong.

Give Us Joy
To Balance Our Affliction

(Psalm 89)

1 O Lord, you have been our refuge
   from one generation to the next.
2 Before the mountains were born
   or the earth or the world brought forth,
   you are God, without beginning or end.

3 You turn men back into dust
   and say: 'Go back, sons of men.'
4 To your eyes a thousand years
   are like yesterday, come and gone,
   no more than a watch in the night.

5 You sweep men away like a dream,
   like grass which springs up in the morning.
6 In the morning it springs up and flowers:
   by evening it withers and fades.

7 So we are destroyed in your anger,
   struck with terror in your fury.
8 Our guilt lies open before you;
   our secrets in the light of your face.

9 All our days pass away in your anger.
   Our life is over like a sigh.
10 Our span is seventy years
   or eighty for those who are strong.

   And most of these are emptiness and pain.
   They pass swiftly and we are gone.

11 Who understands the power of your anger
and fears the strength of your fury?

12 Make us know the shortness of our life
that we may gain wisdom of heart.
13 Lord, relent! Is your anger for ever?
Show pity to your servants.

14 In the morning, fill us with your love;
we shall exult and rejoice all our days.
15 Give us joy to balance our affliction
for the years when we knew misfortune.

16 Show forth your work to your servants;
let your glory shine on their children.
17 Let the favour of the Lord be upon us:
give success to the work of our hands
(give success to the work of our hands).

You, Lord, Have Forgiven

(Psalm 31)

1 Happy the man whose offence is forgiven,
  whose sin is remitted.
2 O happy the man to whom the Lord
  imputes no guilt,
  in whose spirit is no guile.

3 I kept it secret and my frame was wasted.
  I groaned all day long
4 for night and day your hand
  was heavy upon me.
  Indeed, my strength was dried up
  as by the summer's heat.

5 But now I have acknowledged my sins;
  my guilt I did not hide.
  I said: 'I will confess
  my offence to the Lord.'
  And you, Lord, have forgiven
  the guilt of my sin.

6 So let every good man pray to you
  in the time of need.
  The floods of water may reach high
  but him they shall not reach.
7 You are my hiding place, O Lord;
  you save me from distress.
  (You surround me with cries of deliverance.)

*   *   *

8 I will instruct you and teach you
   the way you should go;
   I will give you counsel
   with my eye upon you.

9 Be not like horse and mule, unintelligent,
   needing bridle and bit,
   else they will not approach you.
10 Many sorrows has the wicked
   but he who trusts in the Lord,
   loving mercy surrounds him.

                *   *   *

11 Rejoice, rejoice in the Lord,
   exult, you just!
   O come, ring out your joy,
   all you upright of heart.

Before You All the Earth Shall Bow

(Psalm 65)

1 Cry out with joy to God, all the earth,
2 O sing to the glory of his name.
   O render him glorious praise.
3 Say to God: 'How tremendous your deeds!

Because of the greatness of your strength
your enemies cringe before you.
4 Before you all the earth shall bow;
   shall sing to you, sing to your name!'

5 Come and see the works of God,
   tremendous his deeds among men.
6 He turned the sea into dry land,
   they passed through the river dry-shod.

Let our joy then be in him;
7 he rules for ever by his might.
   His eyes keep watch over the nations:
   let rebels not rise against him.

8 O peoples, bless our God,
   let the voice of his praise resound,
9 of the God who gave life to our souls
   and kept our feet from stumbling.

10 For you, O God, have tested us,
   you have tried us as silver is tried:
11 you led us, God, into the snare;
   you laid a heavy burden on our backs.

12 You let men ride over our heads;
    we went through fire and through water
    but then you brought us relief.

13 Burnt offering I bring to your house;
    to you I will pay my vows,
14 the vows which my lips have uttered,
    which my mouth spoke in my distress.

15 I will offer burnt offerings of fatlings
    with the smoke of burning rams.
    I will offer bullocks and goats.

16 Come and hear, all who fear God.
    I will tell what he did for my soul:
17 to him I cried aloud,
    with high praise ready on my tongue.

18 If there had been evil in my heart,
    the Lord would not have listened.
19 But truly God has listened;
    he has heeded the voice of my prayer.

20 Blessed be God who did not reject my prayer
    nor withhold his love from me.

In God Is My Safety and Glory

(Psalm 61)

2 In God alone is my soul at rest;
my help comes from him.
3 He alone is my rock, my stronghold,
my fortress: I stand firm.

4 How long will you all attack one man
to break him down,
as though he were a tottering wall,
or a tumbling fence?

5 Their plan is only to destroy:
they take pleasure in lies.
With their mouth they utter blessing
but in their heart they curse.

6 In God alone be at rest, my soul;
for my hope comes from him.
7 He alone is my rock, my stronghold,
my fortress: I stand firm.

8 In God is my safety and glory,
the rock of my strength.
Take refuge in God, 9 all you people.
Trust him at all times.
Pour out your hearts before him
for God is our refuge.

10 Common folk are only a breath,
great men an illusion.
Placed in the scales, they rise;
they weigh less than a breath.

11 Do not put your trust in oppression
   nor vain hopes on plunder.
   Do not set your heart on riches
   even when they increase.

12 For God has said only one thing:
   only two do I know:
   that to God alone belongs power
13 and to you, Lord, love;
   and that you repay each man
   according to his deeds.

Do Not Abandon or Forsake Me

(Psalm 26)

1 The Lord is my light and my help;
   whom shall I fear?
   The Lord is the stronghold of my life;
   before whom shall I shrink?

2 When evil-doers draw near
   to devour my flesh,
   it is they, my enemies and foes,
   who stumble and fall.

3 Though an army encamp against me
   my heart would not fear.
   Though war break out against me
   even then would I trust.

4 There is one thing I ask of the Lord,
   for this I long,
   to live in the house of the Lord,
   all the days of my life,
   to savour the sweetness of the Lord,
   to behold his temple.

5 For there he keeps me safe in his tent
   in the day of evil.
   He hides me in the shelter of his tent,
   on a rock he sets me safe.

6 And now my head shall be raised
   above my foes who surround me
   and I shall offer within his tent
   a sacrifice of joy.
   I will sing and make music for the Lord.

7 O Lord, hear my voice when I call;
have mercy and answer.
8 Of you my heart has spoken:
'Seek his face.'

It is your face, O Lord, that I seek;
9 hide not your face.
Dismiss not your servant in anger;
you have been my help.

Do not abandon or forsake me,
O God my help!
10 Though father and mother forsake me,
The Lord will receive me.

11 Instruct me, Lord, in your way;
on an even path lead me.
When they lie in ambush 12 protect me
from my enemy's greed.
False witnesses rise against me,
breathing out fury.

13 I am sure I shall see the Lord's goodness
in the land of the living.
14 Hope in him, hold firm and take heart.
Hope in the Lord!

PART V

**When I Recall Your Promises
and Need To Live in Their Light**

Lord, Who Is Like You?

(Psalm 34)

1 O Lord, plead my cause against my foes;
  fight those who fight me.
2 Take up your buckler and shield;
  arise to help me.

3 Take up the javelin and the spear
  against those who pursue me.
  O Lord, say to my soul:
  'I am your salvation.'

4 Let those who seek my life
  be shamed and disgraced.
  Let those who plan evil against me
  be routed in confusion.

5 Let them be like chaff before the wind;
  let God's angel scatter them.
6 Let their path be slippery and dark;
  let God's angel pursue them.

7 They have hidden a net for me wantonly;
  they have dug a pit.
8 Let ruin fall upon them
  and take them by surprise.
  Let them be caught in the net they have hidden;
  let them fall into their pit.

9 But my soul shall be joyful in the Lord
  and rejoice in his salvation.

10 My whole being will say:
   'Lord, who is like you
   who rescue the weak from the strong
   and the poor from the oppressor?'

11 Lying witnesses arise
   and acuse me unjustly.
12 They repay me evil for good:
   my soul is forlorn.

13 When they were sick I went into mourning,
   afflicted with fasting.
   My prayer was ever on my lips,
14 as for a brother, a friend. ·
   I went as though mourning a mother,
   bowed down with grief.

15 Now that I am in trouble they gather,
   they gather and mock me.
   They take me by surprise and strike me
   and tear me to pieces.
16 They provoke me with mockery on mockery
   and gnash their teeth.

17 O Lord, how long will you look on?
   Come to my rescue!
   Save my life from these raging beasts,
   my soul from these lions.
18 I will thank you in the great assembly,
   amid the throng I will praise you.

19 Do not let my lying foes
   rejoice over me.
   Do not let those who hate me unjustly
   wink eyes at each other.

20 They wish no peace to the peaceful
  who live in the land.
  They make deceitful plots
21 and with mouths wide open
  their cry against me is: 'Yes!
  We saw you do it!'

22 O Lord, you have seen, do not be silent,
  do not stand afar off!
23 Awake, stir to my defence,
  to my cause, O God!

24 Vindicate me, Lord, in your justice,
  do not let them rejoice.
25 Do not let them think: 'Yes! we have won,
  we have brought him to an end!'

26 Let them be shamed and brought to disgrace
  who rejoice at my misfortune.
  Let them be covered with shame and confusion
  who raise themselves against me.

27 Let there be joy for those who love my cause.
  Let them say without end:
  'Great is the Lord who delights
  in the peace of his servant.'
28 Then my tongue shall speak of your justice,
  all day long of your praise.

Open-Handed,
He Gives to the Poor

(Psalm 111)

1 Alleluia!

Happy the man who fears the Lord,
who takes delight in all his commands.
2 His sons will be powerful on earth;
the children of the upright are blessed.

3 Riches and wealth are in his house;
his justice stands firm for ever.
4 He is a light in the darkness for the upright:
he is generous, merciful and just.

5 The good man takes pity and lends,
he conducts his affairs with honour.
6 The just man will never waver:
he will be remembered for ever.

7 He has no fear of evil news;
with a firm heart he trusts in the Lord.
8 With a steadfast heart he will not fear;
he will see the downfall of his foes.

9 Open-handed, he gives to the poor;
his justice stands firm for ever.
His head will be raised in glory.

10 The wicked man sees and is angry,
grinds his teeth and fades away;
the desire of the wicked leads to doom.

You Keep Your Pledge with Wonders

(Psalm 64)

2 To you our praise is due
  in Zion, O God.
  To you we pay our vows,
3 you who hear our prayer.

To you all flesh will come
4 with its burden of sin.
  Too heavy for us, our offences,
  but you wipe them away.

5 Blessed is he whom you choose and call
  to dwell in your courts.
  We are filled with the blessings of your house,
  of your holy temple.

6 You keep your pledge with wonders,
  O God our saviour,
  the hope of all the earth
  and of far distant isles.

7 You uphold the mountains with your strength,
  you are girded with power.
8 You still the roaring of the seas,
  (the roaring of their waves)
  and the tumult of the peoples.

9 The ends of the earth stand in awe
  at the sight of your wonders.

The lands of sunrise and sunset
you fill with your joy.

10 You care for the earth, give it water,
you fill it with riches.
Your river in heaven brims over
to provide its grain.

And thus you provide for the earth;
11 you drench its furrows,
you level it, soften it with showers,
you bless its growth.

12 You crown the year with your goodness.
Abundance flows in your steps,
13 in the pastures of the wilderness it flows.

The hills are girded with joy,
14 the meadows covered with flocks,
the valleys are decked with wheat.
They shout for joy, yes, they sing.

The Lord Gives His Blessing

(Psalm 132)

1 How good and how pleasant it is,
when brothers live in unity!

2 It is like precious oil upon the head
running down upon the beard,
running down upon Aaron's beard,
upon the collar of his robes.

3 It is like the dew of Hermon which falls
on the heights of Zion.
For there the Lord gives his blessing,
life for ever.

The Lord Takes Delight in His People

(Psalm 149)

1 Alleluia!

Sing a new song to the Lord,
his praise in the assembly of the faithful.
2 Let Israel rejoice in its Maker,
let Zion's sons exult in their king.
3 Let them praise his name with dancing
and make music with timbrel and harp.

4 For the Lord takes delight in his people.
He crowns the poor with salvation.
5 Let the faithful rejoice in their glory,
shout for joy and take their rest.

The Lord Guards the Way of the Just

(Psalm 1)

1 Happy indeed is the man
  who follows not the counsel of the wicked;
  nor lingers in the way of sinners
  nor sits in the company of scorners,
2 but whose delight is the law of the Lord
  and who ponders his law day and night.

3 He is like a tree that is planted
  beside the flowing waters,
  that yields its fruit in due season
  and whose leaves shall never fade;
  and all that he does shall prosper.
4 Not so are the wicked, not so!

  For they like winnowed chaff
  shall be driven away by the wind.
5 When the wicked are judged they shall not stand,
  nor find room among those who are just;
6 for the Lord guards the way of the just
  but the way of the wicked leads to doom.

He Is Happy Who Is Helped

(Psalm 145)

1 Alleluia!

My soul, give praise to the Lord;
2 I will praise the Lord all my days,
   make music to my God while I live.

3 Put no trust in princes,
   in mortal men in whom there is no help.
4 Take their breath, they return to clay
   and their plans that day come to nothing.

5 He is happy who is helped by Jacob's God,
   whose hope is in the Lord his God,
6 who alone made heaven and earth,
   the seas and all they contain.

It is he who keeps faith for ever,
7 who is just to those who are oppressed.
It is he who gives bread to the hungry,
the Lord, who sets prisoners free,

8 the Lord who gives sight to the blind,
   who raises up those who are bowed down,
9 the Lord, who protects the stranger
   and upholds the widow and orphan.

8c It is the Lord who loves the just
9c but thwarts the path of the wicked.
10 The Lord will reign for ever,
   Zion's God, from age to age.

Alleluia!

Age to Age Shall Proclaim
Your Works

(Psalm 144)

1 I will give you glory. O God my King,
 I will bless your name for ever.

2 I will bless you day after day
 and praise your name for ever.
3 The Lord is great, highly to be praised,
 his greatness cannot be measured.

4 Age to age shall proclaim your works,
 shall declare your mighty deeds,
5 shall speak of your splendour and glory,
 tell the tale of your wonderful works.
6 They will speak of your terrible deeds,
 recount your greatness and might.
7 They will recall your abundant goodness;
 age to age shall ring out your justice.

8 The Lord is kind and full of compassion,
 slow to anger, abounding in love.
9 How good is the Lord to all,
 compassionate to all his creatures.

10 All your creatures shall thank you, O Lord,
 and your friends shall repeat their blessing.
11 They shall speak of the glory of your reign
 and declare your might, O God,

12 to make known to men your mighty deeds
 and the glorious splendour of your reign.

13 Yours is an everlasting kingdom;
   your rule lasts from age to age.

   The Lord is faithful in all his words
   and loving in all his deeds.
14 The Lord supports all who fall
   and raises all who are bowed down.

15 The eyes of all creatures look to you
   and you give them their food in due time.
16 You open wide your hand,
   grant the desires of all who live.

17 The Lord is just in all his ways
   and loving in all his deeds.
18 He is close to all who call him,
   who call on him from their hearts.

19 He grants the desires of those who fear him,
   he hears their cry and he saves them.
20 The Lord protects all who love him;
   but the wicked he will utterly destroy.

21 Let me speak the praise of the Lord,
   let all mankind bless his holy name
   for ever, for ages unending.

I Have God for My Help

(Psalm 53)

3 O God, save me by your name;
   by your power, uphold my cause.
4 O God, hear my prayer;
   listen to the words of my mouth.

5 For proud men have risen against me,
   ruthless men seek my life.
   They have no regard for God.

6 But I have God for my help.
   The Lord upholds my life.
7 Let the evil recoil upon my foes:
   you who are faithful, destroy them.

8 I will sacrifice to you with willing heart
   and praise your name for it is good:
9 for you have rescued me from all my distress
   and my eyes have seen the downfall of my foes.

They Have Ears
But They Cannot Hear

(Psalm 134)

1 Alleluia!

Praise the name of the Lord,
praise him, servants of the Lord,
2 who stands in the house of the Lord
in the courts of the house of our God.

3 Praise the Lord for the Lord is good.
Sing a psalm to his name for he is loving.
4 For the Lord has chosen Jacob for himself
and Israel for his own possession.

5 For I know the Lord is great,
that our Lord is high above all gods.
6 The Lord does whatever he wills,
in heaven, on earth, in the seas.

7 He summons clouds from the ends of the earth;
makes lightning produce the rain;
from his treasuries he sends forth the wind.

8 The first-born of the Egyptians he smote,
of man and beast alike.
9 Signs and wonders he worked
in the midst of your land, O Egypt,
against Pharaoh and all his servants.

10 Nations in their greatness he struck
and kings in their splendour he slew.

11 Sihon, king of the Amorites,
   Og, the king of Bashan,
   and all the kingdoms of Canaan.
12 He let Israel inherit their land;
   on his people their land he bestowed.

13 Lord, your name stands for ever,
   unforgotten from age to age:
14 for the Lord does justice for his people;
   the Lord takes pity on his servants.

15 Pagan idols are silver and gold,
   the work of human hands.
16 They have mouths but they cannot speak;
   they have eyes but they cannot see.

17 They have ears but they cannot hear;
   there is never a breath on their lips.
18 Their makers will come to be like them
   and so will all who trust in them!

19 Sons of Israel, bless the Lord!
   Sons of Aaron, bless the Lord!
20 Sons of Levi, bless the Lord!
   You who fear him, bless the Lord!

21 From Zion may the Lord be blessed,
   he who dwells in Jerusalem!

Lord, Come to My Rescue

(Psalm 39)

2 I waited, I waited for the Lord
   and he stooped down to me;
   he heard my cry.

3 He drew me from the deadly pit,
   from the miry clay.
   He set my feet upon a rock
   and made my footsteps firm.

4 He put a new song into my mouth,
   praise of our God.
   Many shall see and fear
   and shall trust in the Lord.

5 Happy the man who has placed
   his trust in the Lord
   and has not gone over to the rebels
   who follow false gods.

6 How many, O Lord my God,
   are the wonders and designs
   that you have worked for us;
   you have no equal.
   Should I proclaim and speak of them,
   they are more than I can tell!

7 You do not ask for sacrifice and offerings,
   but an open ear.
   You do not ask for holocaust and victim.
8 Instead, here am I.

In the scroll of the book it stands written
9 that I should do your will.
My God, I delight in your law
in the depth of my heart.

10 Your justice I have proclaimed
in the great assembly.
My lips I have not sealed;
you know it, O Lord.

12 O Lord, you will not withhold
your compassion from me.
Your merciful love and your truth
will always guard me.

13 For I am beset with evils
too many to be counted.
My sins have fallen upon me
and my sight fails me.
They are more than the hairs of my head
and my heart sinks.

14 O Lord, come to my rescue,
Lord, come to my aid.
15 O let there be shame and confusion
on those who seek my life.

O let them turn back in confusion,
who delight in my harm.
16 Let them be appalled, covered with shame,
who jeer at my lot.

17 O let there be rejoicing and gladness
for all who seek you.

Let them ever say: 'The Lord is great',
who love your saving help.

18 As for me, wretched and poor,
the Lord thinks of me.
You are my rescuer, my help,
O God, do not delay.

He Remembered His Holy Word

(Psalm 104)

Alleluia!

1 Give thanks to the Lord, tell his name,
make known his deeds among the peoples.

2 O sing to him, sing his praise;
tell all his wonderful works!
3 Be proud of his holy name,
let the hearts that seek the Lord rejoice.

4 Consider the Lord and his strength;
constantly seek his face.
5 Remember the wonders he has done,
his miracles, the judgments he spoke.

6 O children of Abraham, his servant,
O sons of the Jacob he chose.
7 He, the Lord, is our God:
his judgments prevail in all the earth.

8 He remembers his covenant for ever,
his promise for a thousand generations,
9 the covenant he made with Abraham,
the oath he swore to Isaac.

10 He confirmed it for Jacob as a law,
for Israel as a covenant for ever.
11 He said: 'I am giving you a land,
Canaan, your appointed heritage.'

12 When they were few in number,
    a handful of strangers in the land,
13 when they wandered from country to country,
    from one kingdom and nation to another,

14 he allowed no one to oppress them;
    he admonished kings on their account:
15 'Do not touch those I have anointed;
    do no harm to any of my prophets.'

16 But he called down a famine on the land;
    he broke the staff that supported them.
17 He had sent a man before them,
    Joseph, sold as a slave.

18 His feet were put in chains,
    his neck was bound with iron,
19 until what he said came to pass
    and the word of the Lord proved him true.

20 Then the king sent and released him;
    the ruler of the peoples set him free,
21 making him master of his house
    and ruler of all he possessed,

22 to instruct his princes as he pleased
    and to teach his elders wisdom.
23 So Israel came into Egypt,
    Jacob lived in the country of Ham.

24 He gave his people increase;
    he made them stronger than their foes,
25 whose hearts he turned to hate his people
    and to deal deceitfully with his servants.

26 Then he sent Moses his servant
   and Aaron the man he had chosen.
27 Through them he showed his marvels
   and his wonders in the country of Ham.

28 He sent darkness, and dark was made
   but Egypt resisted his words.
29 He turned the waters into blood
   and caused their fish to die.

30 Their land was alive with frogs,
   even in the halls of their kings.
31 He spoke; the dog-fly came
   and gnats covered the land.

32 He sent hail-stones in place of the rain
   and flashing fire in their land.
33 He struck their vines and fig-trees;
   he shattered the trees through their land.

34 He spoke; the locusts came,
   young locusts, too many to be counted.
35 They ate up every blade in the land;
   they ate up all the fruit of their fields.

36 He struck all the first-born in their land,
   the finest flower of their sons.
37 He led out Israel with silver and gold.
   In his tribes were none who fell behind.

38 Egypt rejoiced when they left
   for dread had fallen upon them.
39 He spread a cloud as a screen
   and fire to give light in the darkness.

40 When they asked for food he sent quails;
   he filled them with bread from heaven.
41 He pierced the rock to give them water;
   it gushed forth in the desert like a river.

42 For he remembered his holy word,
   which he gave to Abraham his servant.
43 So he brought out his people with joy,
   his chosen ones with shouts of rejoicing.

44 And he gave them the land of the nations.
   They took the fruit of other men's toil,
45 that thus they might keep his precepts,
   that thus they might observe his laws.

Alleluia!

Long Ago
You Founded the Earth

(Psalm 101)

2 O Lord, listen to my prayer
   and let my cry for help reach you.
3 Do not hide your face from me
   in the day of my distress.
   Turn your ear towards me
   and answer me quickly when I call.

4 For my days are vanishing like smoke,
   my bones burn away like a fire.
5 My heart is withered like the grass.
   I forget to eat my bread.
6 I cry with all my strength
   and my skin clings to my bones.

7 I have become like a pelican in the wilderness,
   like an owl in desolate places.
8 I lie awake and I moan
   like some lonely bird on a roof.
9 All day long my foes revile me;
   those who hate me use my name as a curse.

10 The bread I eat is ashes;
    my drink is mingled with tears.
11 In your anger, Lord, and your fury
    you have lifted me up and thrown me down.
12 My days are like a passing shadow
    and I wither away like the grass.

*   *   *

13 But you, O Lord, will endure for ever*

and your name from age to age.
14 You will arise and have mercy on Zion:
for this is the time to have mercy,
(yes, the time appointed has come)
15 for your servants love her very stones,
are moved with pity even for her dust.

16 The nations shall fear the name of the Lord
and all the earth's kings your glory,
17 when the Lord shall build up Zion again
and appear in all his glory.
18 Then he will turn to the prayers of the helpless;
he will not despise their prayers.

19 Let this be written for ages to come
that a people yet unborn may praise the Lord;
20 for the Lord leaned down from his sanctuary on
high.
He looked down from heaven to the earth
21 that he might hear the groans of the prisoners
and free those condemned to die.

29 The sons of your servants shall dwell untroubled
and their race shall endure before you
22 that the name of the Lord may be proclaimed in
Zion
and his praise in the heart of Jerusalem,
23 when peoples and kingdoms are gathered together
to pay their homage to the Lord.

*   *   *

24 He has broken my strength in mid-course;
he has shortened the days of my life.

25 I say to God: 'Do not take me away
    before my days are complete,
    you, whose days last from age to age.

26 Long ago you founded the earth
    and the heavens are the work of your hands.
27 They will perish but you will remain.
    They will all wear out like a garment.
    You will change them like clothes that are changed.
28 But you neither change, nor have an end.'

When, Lord, Will You Come?

(Psalm 100)

1 My song is of mercy and justice;
   I sing to you, O Lord.
2 I will walk in the way of perfection.
   O when, Lord, will you come?

   I will walk with blameless heart
   within my house;
3 I will not set before my eyes
   whatever is base.

   I will hate the ways of the crooked;
   they shall not be my friends.
4 The false-hearted must keep far away;
   the wicked I disown.

5 The man who slanders his neighbour in secret
   I will bring to silence.
   The man of proud looks and haughty heart
   I will never endure.

6 I look to the faithful in the land
   that they may dwell with me.
   He who walks in the way of perfection
   shall be my friend.

7 No man who practises deceit
   shall live within my house.
   No man who utters lies shall stand
   before my eyes.

8 Morning by morning I will silence
   all the wicked in the land,
   uprooting from the city of the Lord
   all who do evil.

You Will Give Me Back My Life

(Psalm 70)

1 In you, O Lord, I take refuge;
   let me never be put to shame.
2 In your justice rescue me, free me:
   pay heed to me and save me.

3 Be a rock where I can take refuge,
   a mighty stronghold to save me;
   for you are my rock, my stronghold.
4 Free me from the hand of the wicked,
   from the grip of the unjust, of the oppressor.

5 It is you, O Lord, who are my hope,
   my trust, O Lord, since my youth.
6 On you I have leaned from my birth,
   from my mother's womb you have been my help.
   My hope has always been in you.

7 My fate has filled many with awe
   but you are my strong refuge.
8 My lips are filled with your praise,
   with your glory all the day long.
9 Do not reject me now that I am old;
   when my strength fails do not forsake me.

10 For my enemies are speaking about me;
    those who watch me take counsel together
11 saying: 'God has forsaken him; follow him,
    seize him; there is no one to save him.'

12 O God, do not stay far off:
   my God, make haste to help me!

13 Let them be put to shame and destroyed,
   all those who seek my life.
   Let them be covered with shame and confusion,
   all those who seek to harm me.

14 But as for me, I will always hope
   and praise you more and more.
15 My lips will tell of your justice
   and day by day of your help
   (though I can never tell it all).

16 I will declare the Lord's mighty deeds
   proclaiming your justice, yours alone.
17 O God, you have taught me from my youth
   and I proclaim your wonders still.

18 Now that I am old and grey-headed,
   do not forsake me, God.
   Let me tell of your power to all ages,
   praise your strength 19 and justice to the skies,
   tell of you who have worked such wonders.
   O God, who is like you?

20 You have burdened me with bitter troubles
   but you will give me back my life.
   You will raise me from the depths of the earth;
21 you will exalt me and console me again.

22 So I will give you thanks on the lyre
   for your faithful love, my God.
   To you will I sing with the harp,
   to you, the Holy One of Israel.

23 When I sing to you my lips shall rejoice
   and my soul, which you have redeemed.

24 And all the day long my tongue
   shall tell the tale of your justice:
   for they are put to shame and disgraced,
   all those who seek to harm me.

Let Them Say For Ever: "God Is Great"

(Psalm 69)

2 O God, make haste to my rescue,
Lord, come to my aid!
3 Let there be shame and confusion
on those who seek my life.

O let them turn back in confusion,
who delight in my harm,
4 let them retreat, covered with shame,
who jeer at my lot.

5 Let there be rejoicing and gladness
for all who seek you.
Let them say for ever: 'God is great,'
who love your saving help.

6 As for me, wretched and poor,
come to me, O God.
You are my rescuer, my help,
O Lord, do not delay.

He Shows the Path
to Those Who Stray

(Psalm 24)

1 To you, O Lord, I lift up my soul.
2 I trust you, let me not be disappointed;
   do not let my enemies triumph.
3 Those who hope in you shall not be disappointed,
   but only those who wantonly break faith.

4 Lord, make me know your ways.
   Lord, teach me your paths.
5 Make me walk in your truth, and teach me:
   for you are God my saviour.

   In you I hope all day long
7c because of your goodness, O Lord.
6 Remember your mercy, Lord,
   and the love you have shown from of old.
7 Do not remember the sins of my youth.
   In your love remember me.

8 The Lord is good and upright.
   He shows the path to those who stray,
9 He guides the humble in the right path;
   He teaches his way to the poor.

10 His ways are faithfulness and love
   for those who keep his covenant and will.
11 Lord, for the sake of your name
   forgive my guilt; for it is great.

12 If anyone fears the Lord
   he will show him the path he should choose.
13 His soul shall live in happiness
   and his children shall possess the land.
14 The Lord's friendship is for those who revere him;
   to them he reveals his covenant.

15 My eyes are always on the Lord;
   for he rescues my feet from the snare.
16 Turn to me and have mercy
   for I am lonely and poor.

17 Relieve the anguish of my heart
   and set me free from my distress.
18 See my affliction and my toil
   and take all my sins away.

19 See how many are my foes;
   how violent their hatred for me.
20 Preserve my life and rescue me.
   Do not disappoint me, you are my refuge.
21 May innocence and uprightness protect me:
   for my hope is in you, O Lord.

22 Redeem Israel, O God, from all its distress.

Who Is the King of Glory?

(Psalm 23)

1 The Lord's is the earth and its fullness,
the world and all its peoples.
2 It is he who set it on the seas;
on the waters he made it firm.

3 Who shall climb the mountain of the Lord?
Who shall stand in his holy place?
4 The man with clean hands and pure heart,
who desires not worthless things,
(who has not sworn so as to deceive his neighbour.)

5 He shall receive blessings from the Lord
and reward from the God who saves him.
6 Such are the men who seek him,
seek the face of the God of Jacob.

* * *

7 O gates, lift high your heads;
grow higher, ancient doors.
Let him enter, the king of glory!

8 Who is the king of glory?
The Lord, the mighty, the valiant,
the Lord, the valiant in war.

9 O gates, lift high your heads;
grow higher, ancient doors.
Let him enter, the king of glory!

10 Who is he, the king of glory?
He, the Lord of armies,
he is the king of glory.